# I Like to Draw!

# MONSTERS

## and

# OTHER MYTHICAL CREATURES

by Rochelle Baltzer    Illustrated by James Penfield

Looking Glass Library

An Imprint of Magic Wagon
www.abdopublishing.com

**www.abdopublishing.com**

Published by Magic Wagon, a division of ABDO, PO Box 398166, Minneapolis, Minnesota 55439. Copyright © 2015 by Abdo Consulting Group, Inc. International copyrights reserved in all countries. No part of this book may be reproduced in any form without written permission from the publisher. Looking Glass Library™ is a trademark and logo of Magic Wagon.

Printed in the United States of America, North Mankato, Minnesota.
102014
012015

 THIS BOOK CONTAINS RECYCLED MATERIALS

Cover and Interior Elements and Photos: iStockphoto, Scott Brundage, Thinkstock

Written by Rochelle Baltzer
Illustrations by James Penfield
Edited by Tamara L. Britton, Bridget O' Brien
Cover and interior design by Candice Keimig

**Library of Congress Cataloging-in-Publication Data**

Baltzer, Rochelle, 1982- author.
   Monsters and other mythical creatures / written by Rochelle Baltzer ; illustrated by James Penfield.
      pages cm -- (I like to draw!)
   Includes index.
   ISBN 978-1-62402-083-4
1. Monsters in art--Juvenile literature. 2. Animals, Mythical, in art--Juvenile literature. 3. Drawing--Technique--Juvenile literature. I. Penfield, James, illustrator. II. Title.
   NC825.M6B35 2015
   743.8'7--dc23
                            2014037676

FLAP FLAP

Dragons Rule!
Unicorns drool!

Roar Roar!
Roar Roar!
Roar Roar!

# TABLE of CONTENTS

# MONSTERS and OTHER MYTHICAL CREATURES

From the walking dead to bloodthirsty beasts, monsters lurk in the shadows and creep their way into our minds. Mythical creatures, such as three-headed dogs and fire-breathing dragons, are equally fascinating. Let your imagination run wild as you learn to draw some of the most awesome monsters and mythical creatures!

# STUFF YOU'LL NEED

Pencil

Paper

Eraser

Marker

Colored Pencils

# KNOW THE BASICS

## SHAPES

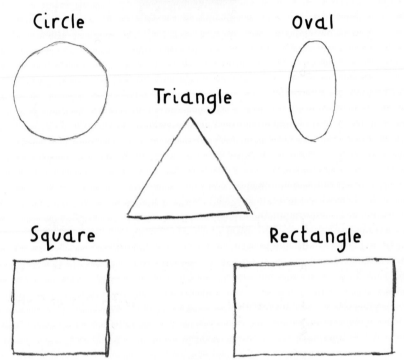

Circle

Oval

Triangle

Square

Rectangle

## LINES
### thick & thin

Straight

Wavy

Jagged

# TALK LIKE AN ARTIST

## Composition

Composition is the way parts of a drawing or picture are arranged. Balanced composition means having an even amount of parts, such as lines and shapes.

Unbalanced

Balanced

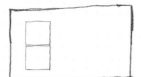

## Dimension

Dimension is the amount of space an object takes up. Drawings are created on a flat surface and have length and width but not depth. So, they are two-dimensional. You can give an object depth by layering colors and adding shadow. This makes it look like it's popping off the page!

Without Dimension

With Dimension

## Shadow

Shadow is created by the way light shines on an object. Look outside on a sunny day. See how the sunlight shines on a tree? The side of the tree with more sunlight appears lighter than the other side.

Without Shadow

With Shadow

# WEREWOLF

*Hoooooowl* . . . According to legend, a werewolf is a man who turns into a wolf at night, often during a full moon. Werewolves have incredible strength. With sharp claws and razor-like teeth, these monsters **devour** animals and even people. At dawn, they change back into their human form.

**1** Draw a circle for the head, shapes for the jaws, and an oval for the body.

**2** Add lines for the arms and legs. Draw in the tail.

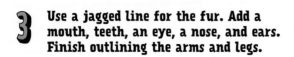

**3** Use a jagged line for the fur. Add a mouth, teeth, an eye, a nose, and ears. Finish outlining the arms and legs.

**4** Add claws to the hands and feet, and finish the mouth. Add more jagged lines on the body to give the fur shape and dimension.

## ART TIP
Adding more jagged lines to the werewolf's fur gives it texture. Experiment with those lines to make the wolf's coat look very furry or less furry!

**5** Outline the finished drawing with a thin, black marker.

**6** Wolves can be black, gray, brown, white, or a variation of those, so give your werewolf one of these fur coats!

## Fear Factor
In some countries, this legendary monster is a man changed into another fearsome animal. It can be a bear, tiger, or hyena.

# VAMPIRE

At night, they emerge from their coffins to drink human blood. Vampires have appeared in horror stories for hundreds of years. These **ghoulish** monsters have pale skin and sharp fangs, which they use to bite the necks of sleeping humans. Once bitten, a human dies and becomes a vampire.

**1** Draw an oval for the head and a larger oval for the body. Outline the cape.

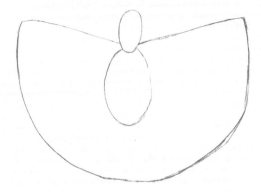

**2** Add lines for legs and arms. Draw ears and the collar of the cape behind the head.

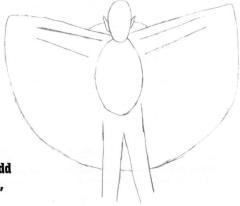

**3** Give the cape definition. Draw the vampire's eyes, nose, mouth, and fangs. Add some hair. Draw a suit, a vest underneath, and a bow tie. Don't forget to add shoes!

**4** Add a necklace to this vampire's chest. Give the cape more definition, and add buttons to the vest. Also add lines for the cheekbones.

## ART TIP

Red advances and purple recedes, so these colors work great for the vampire's vest and cape. Or, choose two shades of a different color to get the same effect!

**5** Outline the finished drawing with a thin, black marker.

**6** Vampires are called "creatures of the night." So typically we think of them dressed in black. But, feel free to use whatever colors you wish!

Repellent that Reeks
Garlic is said to keep away vampires.

# BIGFOOT

Have you heard stories about Bigfoot? Sightings are most common in the mountains of California, Oregon, and Washington. This massive, apelike monster is covered in dark hair, walks upright, and smells foul. Its screeches and howls pierce the quiet forest. Its footprints measure up to 24 inches (60 cm) long!

**1** Draw a large oval for the body and a smaller one for the head.

**2** Add lines for the arms and legs. It already looks like it's walking!

**3** Give your Bigfoot a furry coat by drawing a jagged line to outline the head and body. Leave the face, hands, chest, and feet uncovered. Draw in the face.

**4** Add lines around the face to show longer hair. Give the body fur detail by drawing more jagged lines. Add chest muscles. Draw in fingernails and toenails.

**5** Outline the finished drawing with a thin, black marker.

**6** To remain unseen, Bigfoot needs to blend into its forest home. Think of the colors of trees, rocks, and dirt. Brown seems to be a good fit!

**Name Game**
Bigfoot is known by other names around the world. These include Sasquatch, Yeti, and Abominable Snowman.

13

# SEA SERPENT

The Loch Ness Monster, or Nessie, is a famous sea serpent. Nessie has a long neck, a small head, a large body, and flippers. People report seeing dark humps rise above the surface of a lake. Other sea serpent sightings have been described as snakelike. But is it real or an **illusion**?

**1** Draw a small circle for the head, a large oval for the body, and curved lines for the neck to connect them. Also add a shape for the snout.

**2** Begin to outline the flippers extending out from the body. Add a tail.

**3** Finish the flippers and add a top and bottom jaw to the head.

**4** Add more details to the face and head. Draw an eye, a nostril, and teeth.

**5** Outline the finished drawing with a thin, black marker.

**6** Sea serpents are bound to come in many different colors depending on where they're swimming! Think about where yours will be swimming and color it to match its environment!

## Age-old Monsters

Asian myths describe dragons under the sea. The Bible also describes a giant sea serpent.

# ZOMBIE

Zombies are dead, rotting bodies that walk the earth. These monsters move slowly, as if in a **trance**, and they do not talk. They feel no pain, and they attack living people. Zombie legends describe people using magic to bring dead bodies to life and make them do evil things.

**1** Draw three ovals for the head, body, and hips. Add lines for the neck.

**2** Give this zombie arms and legs by starting the outlines.

**3** Draw in the face and add some hair. Outline the rest of the body, and add a thought bubble coming from the head.

**4** Add fingers and toes. Draw wavy and jagged lines to add texture to the hair. Make jagged lines for tears in the pants and shirt. Finally, write "MMMM . . . BRAINS" in the thought bubble to let everyone know this zombie's favorite food!

**5** Outline the finished drawing with a thin, black marker.

**6** Zombies come in all shapes, sizes, and colors. Be creative and think about what colors your zombie might be wearing. Have fun with it!

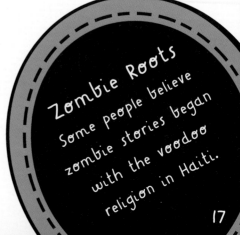

Zombie Roots
Some people believe zombie stories began with the voodoo religion in Haiti.

# CHUPACABRA

Is it a dog? A lizard? An alien? Chupacabra (choo-pa-KAHB-ruh) reports vary. Some are described as having wings. Others are said to have **quills** running down their spines. Witnesses say this monster has a hairless back, long claws, and sharp fangs! Sightings are most common in the Southwest, especially Texas.

**1** Draw a circle for the head, a shape for the snout, and an oval for the body.

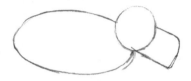

**2** Draw lines for the arms and legs and a skinny, curvy tail.

**3** Outline the rest of the arms, legs, and body. Add ears and draw in the face. Include the eyes, nose, mouth, and sharp teeth!

**4** Add spikes to the chupacabra's back, and give it some claws.

## ART TIP
Whenever you're drawing something repetitive, like the spikes on this creature's back, draw each shape a little different for a more natural look.

**5** Outline the finished drawing with a thin, black marker.

**6** People say the chupacabra is brown. Color the eyes yellow or whatever other menacing color you can think of!

### Bloodthirsty Beasts
Chupacabra means "goat sucker" in Spanish. This monster got its name because it is said to attack livestock and drink their blood.

# CERBERUS

Cerberus (SUHR-buh-ruhs) is a three-headed dog with a snake's tail. In Greek and Roman myths, this creature guards the entrance to the underworld. He keeps the living from entering and the dead from leaving.

**1** Draw three circles for the heads and three ovals for the body. Add shapes for the jaws on the heads.

**2** Add lines for the legs and the tail.

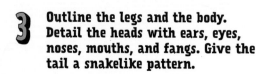

**3** Outline the legs and the body. Detail the heads with ears, eyes, noses, mouths, and fangs. Give the tail a snakelike pattern.

**4** Add claws to the feet. Give dimension to the ears and heads.

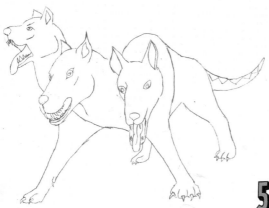

**ART TIP**

You can make each head of Cerberus look different. They can all look mean and ferocious, or just one! It's up to you!

**5** Outline the finished drawing with a thin, black marker.

**6** Cerberus can be any color a dog can be! Keep in mind its snake tail when adding color.

**Dog Charmer**

Mythical hero Orpheus is said to have gotten past Cerberus by playing music.

# CENTAUR

A centaur (SEHN-tawr) has the upper body of a man and the lower body of a horse. In Greek myths, centaurs are violent and uncivilized. They fight using tree branches as weapons. Chiron is a well-known mythical centaur. Unlike other centaurs, he is regarded as wise.

**1** Draw a circle for the head, an oval for the upper body, and an oval for the lower body.

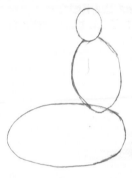

**2** Add lines for the arms and legs. Also draw a tail and outline the horns.

**3** Draw a face and some spiky hair! Finish outlining the arms and legs. Add arm bands to the arms. Draw a jagged line to show the line between the horse body and the human body.

**4** Draw knuckles on the hands. Add detail to the horns. Draw the hooves. Then, give this centaur some muscles!

**ART TIP**
Lines slanted downward over the eyes make your centaur look mean and nasty, like it's scowling!

**5** Outline the finished drawing with a thin, black marker.

**6** Play around with color choices. Horses come in many colors. Be adventurous! You could add spots to your centaur's horse body.

**Centaurs at Hogwarts** Centaurs appear in the Harry Potter books. Some live in the Forbidden Forest.

# UNICORN

Unicorns have appeared in folktales since ancient times. Thousands of years ago, a Greek doctor described a donkey-like animal he saw in India. It had a white body, blue eyes, and a horn on its forehead. Today, most unicorns are shown as large, white horses with a **spiraling** horn.

**1** Draw a circle for the head, shapes for the neck and snout, and an oval for the body.

**2** Add lines for the legs and tail.

**3** Finish outlining the body, legs, and tail. Draw eyes, a mouth, and the unicorn's famous horn. Also add ears and a flowing mane.

**4** Finish the horn by adding spirals to it. Detail the ears and snout, and outline the hooves.

### ART TIP
To give your unicorn a wild, flowing mane and tail, use a loose, wavy line to outline the hair.

**5** Outline the finished drawing with a thin, black marker.

**6** A unicorn's mane and tail are colorful and bright. Choose bright colors to add life to your unicorn!

### Special Power
In the Middle Ages, cups said to have been made from unicorn horn were believed to protect against poisoned drinks.

25

# DRAGON

A dragon is an enormous, lizard-like creature. It beats its bat-like wings and slashes enemies with its large tail. This mythical animal has sharp teeth and breathes fire! In European folktales, dragons are feared and often slew. But in Asian legends, they represent wealth and luck.

**1** Draw a circle for the head, a shape for the snout, and an oval for the body.

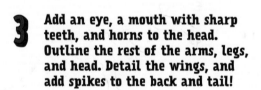

**2** Add lines for the arms and legs. Draw the tail and the wings.

**3** Add an eye, a mouth with sharp teeth, and horns to the head. Outline the rest of the arms, legs, and head. Detail the wings, and add spikes to the back and tail!

**4** Finish the arms and legs, and add claws. Add nose holes and lines on the head to give it dimension.

**ART TIP**
You could draw the dragon breathing fire if you want to add action to your art!

**5** Outline the finished drawing with a thin, black marker.

**6** Typically people think of dragons being green, but be creative! Color your dragon a fierce red or a soft and mellow light purple to change its character.

**Treasure Trove**
In European **medieval** stories, a dragon often guards treasure. The person who slays the dragon gains the treasure.

27

# Fact and Fantasy

Count Dracula is a famous vampire described in the **1897** book by Bram Stoker.

Bigfoot **is depicted on American Indian** totem poles.

Kraken **is a** sea monster **from Norwegian myths. Stories describe the giant creature devouring whales and ships.**

**The** chupacabra **legend began in the 1990s in Puerto Rico. Farmers found dead livestock with puncture wounds in their necks.**

**Chinese New Year's Day parades feature a large** dragon **costume. It is said to** prevent evil **from coming into the new year.**

Unicorns **stand for** purity **and** love **in European legends.**

# Glossary

**devour** (dih-VAWR) – to eat quickly, showing hunger.

**ghoulish** (GOO-lihsh) – like a ghoul, which is an evil being that eats dead bodies.

**illusion** – something that is not real but seems real.

**medieval** (mih-DEE-vuhl) – of or relating to the Middle Ages.

**Middle Ages** – a time in European history from about the 500s to the 1500s.

**quill** – a large, stiff feather or a sharp spine.

**spiraling** – winding around a central point, while moving closer to or farther away from it.

**trance** – a state that is like being asleep except you are able to move like a person who is awake.

# Websites

To learn more about I Like to Draw!, visit **booklinks.abdopublishing.com**. These links are routinely monitored and updated to provide the most current information available.

# Index